TRAVEL WITH THE GREAT EXPLORERS

Explore with

Vasco Núñez de Balboa

Meredith Dault

Crabtree Publishing Company
www.crabtreebooks.com

Crabtree Publishing Company
www.crabtreebooks.com

Author: Meredith Dault

Managing Editor: Tim Cooke

Designer: Lynne Lennon

Picture Manager: Sophie Mortimer

Design Manager: Keith Davis

Editorial Director: Lindsey Lowe

Children's Publisher: Anne O'Daly

Crabtree Editorial Director: Kathy Middleton

Crabtree Editor: Petrice Custance

Proofreader: Angela Kaelberer

**Production coordinator
and prepress technician:** Tammy McGarr

Print coordinator: Margaret Amy Salter

Written and produced for Crabtree Publishing Company
by Brown Bear Books

Photographs:
Front Cover: **Dreamstime:** Rodrigo Cuel tr; **Shutterstock:** br;
Thinkstock: istockphoto cr; **Topfoto:** The Image Works main.

Interior: Alamy: Arco Images GmbH 24, Chronicle 10br, Julio Etchart 20, Victor Santamaria Gonzalez 21l, Peter Horee 25b, Georgias Kollidas 19b, North Wind Picture Archives 5c, 11l, 19t, 26bl, Pictorial Press Ltd 28b, Prisma Archivo 14, David Woodfall/Avalon 17br; **Dreamstime:** 12t, Jesse Kraft 23t; **Getty Images:** Imagno 27cl, Eric Lafforgue/Art in All of Us 21r; **istockphoto:** 13b; **Public Domain:** 11r, Bancroft Library, University
of California 6, Kimon Berlin/Gribeco 15l, Real Academia de Ballas Artes de San Fernando 27br; **Shutterstock:** Gualtiero Boffi 5br, Svetlana Bykova 16, B. Campbell 26cr, Coloa Studio 22r, Viktar Miyshchyts 23br; **Thinkstock:** Johannes Compaan 22-23b, David Evison 25t, istockphoto 17l, Maribel Ortega 4bl; **Topfoto:** Granger Collection 7b, 12b, 18, 28t, Image Works 4, 10, 13t, 15r, 29, Roger-Viollet 7t.
All other artwork and maps, **Brown Bear Books Ltd.**

Brown Bear Books has made every attempt to contact the copyright holder. If you have any information please contact licensing@brownbearbooks.co.uk

Library and Archives Canada Cataloguing in Publication

CIP Available at the Library and Archives Canada

Library of Congress Cataloging-in-Publication Data

Names: Dault, Meredith, author.
Title: Explore with Vasco Nunez de Balboa / Meredith Dault.
Description: New York : Crabtree Publishing Company, 2018. |
 Series: Travel with the Great Explorers | Includes and index.
 | Audience: Grades 4-6. | Audience: Ages 8-11.
Identifiers: LCCN 2017028417 (print) | LCCN 2017028922 (ebook) |
 ISBN 9781427178114 (Electronic HTML) |
 ISBN 9780778739210 (reinforced library binding : alk. paper) |
 ISBN 9780778739272 (pbk. : alk. paper)
Subjects: LCSH: Balboa, Vasco Núñez de, 1475-1519--Juvenile literature. |
 Explorers--America--Biography--Juvenile literature. |
 Explorers--Spain--Biography--Juvenile literature. | America--Discovery and
 exploration--Spanish--Juvenile literature.
Classification: LCC E125.B2 (ebook) | LCC E125.B2 D38 2018 (print) |
 DDC 910.92 [B] --dc23
LC record available at https://lccn.loc.gov/2017028417

Crabtree Publishing Company
www.crabtreebooks.com   1-800-387-7650

Printed in Canada/092017/PB20170719

Published in Canada
Crabtree Publishing
616 Welland Ave.
St. Catharines, ON
L2M 5V6

Published in the United States
Crabtree Publishing
PMB 59051
350 Fifth Avenue, 59th Floor
New York, New York 10118

Published in the United Kingdom
Crabtree Publishing
Maritme House
Basin Road North, Hove
BN41 1WR

Published in Australia
Crabtree Publishing
3 Charles Street
Coburg North
VIC, 3058

CONTENTS

Meet the Boss

Vasco Núñez de Balboa was a young man in Spain when Christopher Columbus sailed to the Americas in 1492. Like many young Spaniards, Balboa dreamed of seeking his fortune abroad in this "New World."

SPANISH CHILDHOOD

+ Poor prospects

Vasco Núñez de Balboa was born in around 1475 in the village of Jerez de los Caballeros, Spain. His family came from the **nobility** but had little money, so Balboa had few **prospects**. After Columbus claimed the New World on behalf of Spain, Balboa decided to try his luck there. In 1500 he joined a voyage commanded by Rodrigo de Bastidas to explore the coasts of what are now Colombia and Panama.

IMPRESSIVE INDIVIDUAL

★ **Love of adventure**

★ **Good at making friends**

Contemporary accounts say that Balboa was strong, energetic, and popular. He was widely respected for his honesty, intelligence, and courage. In his first voyage to Colombia (left) with Bastidas, Balboa learned quickly how to get along with the **Indigenous** peoples. This ability would help him in his later explorations.

IN SANTO DOMINGO

★ **Adventurer settles down**

★ **Proves a poor farmer**

At the end of his voyage to Colombia and Panama, Balboa decided not to return to Spain. He settled in Santo Domingo in the Spanish **colony** of Hispaniola (below), in the modern-day Dominican Republic. He received some land in return for his voyage with Bastidas, but he was a bad farmer and soon found himself in debt to other Spaniards on the island.

My Explorer Journal

★ **Imagine that you are Balboa. Write a letter to the Spanish authorities in Santo Domingo to explain why you should be allowed to sail to Panama despite your debts.**

> He was capable of any degree of **fatigue**. His was the strongest lance, his was the surest arrow in the company." *A Spanish biographer describes Balboa.*

A CHANCE TO FLEE

+ A possible way out

In 1510, Balboa heard about an expedition heading to Darién, on the coast of Panama. The expedition was being led by Martín Fernández de Enciso, and Balboa wanted to join him. However, the people he owed money to in Santo Domingo asked the Spanish authorities to prevent him from going. The authorities ordered Fernández de Enciso not to take anyone on the voyage who was in debt in Hispaniola.

SMUGGLED ON BOARD!

☞ **Hidden in a barrel**

Balboa was determined to join Encisco's expedition. He **bribed** some men to smuggle him onto the ship. Balboa climbed inside an empty barrel, together with his dog, Leoncico. The men carried the barrel onto the ship with the other supplies. Balboa only appeared from the barrel once the ship was too far from Santo Domingo to turn back.

Where Are We Heading?

Did you know ?

Balboa sailed to a group of small islands in the Pacific about 30 miles (48 km) off the coast of Panama. He called them the Pearl Islands because of their many oyster beds.

In Panama, Balboa proved to be a natural and brave leader. When he heard stories of a vast ocean unknown to Europeans, he became determined to reach it.

SANTA MARIA DE LA ANTIGUA DEL DARIÉN

☞ **Founding a colony**

When Balboa reached Darién in 1510, he found the Spanish colony there under attack from Indigenous peoples. He founded a new colony, Santa Maria de la Antigua del Darién, on the Gulf of Urabá, usually just called Darién. The village grew to become the first permanent European settlement in Central America, with more than 200 **thatched** huts. Eventually Balboa became the settlement's leader.

LAND BRIDGE

+ A difficult journey

The **Isthmus** of Panama is the narrow land bridge that connects North and South America. At its narrowest, only 31 miles (50 km) divides the Atlantic Ocean to the northeast from the Pacific Ocean to the southwest. Balboa was the first European to make the crossing. Hearing stories of an unknown sea to the south from Indigenous peoples, Balboa set out to find it with nearly 200 soldiers and many local

HEIGHTS OF DARIÉN

+ A southern ocean

On September 25, 1513, Balboa and his dog, Leoncico, climbed a mountain in the middle of Panama. In the distance was a blue sea. Balboa had become the first European to see the Pacific Ocean from the New World. Balboa and his companions celebrated by building a stone altar and erecting a cross. He claimed the whole of what he named the South Sea. He even had his claim written down and witnessed by a **notary** in order to make it official.

Weather Forecast

DRAINING HEAT

Balboa's route to the Pacific led through thick jungles, across swamps, and over steep mountain ranges. The journey was made more difficult by the constant heat and humidity. Even slight activity was exhausting.

TRAVEL UPDATE

Reaching the Water

★ If you ever discover somewhere new, remember to claim it. On September 29, 1513, Balboa reached the South Sea. Wearing his full armor, he walked into the water up to his knees (left). He claimed the whole ocean for the King of Spain—even though its coasts and islands were already well populated!

BALBOA'S EXPLORATIONS IN PANAMA

Balboa and his men are best known for their journey across the Isthmus of Panama to reach the Pacific Ocean. In fact, Balboa made the journey to the Pacific twice, and explored the Pearl Islands there.

Belize

Guatemala

Honduras

El Salvador

Nicaragua

Costa Rica

Panama

Careta

Tumaco   Darién

PACIFIC OCEAN

Pearl Islands
Balboa built boats so that he could sail to these islands off the Pacific coast of Panama. They were a rich source of pearls, which were very valuable in Spain. Today, the islands are known as Las Perlas, the Pearl Islands.

San Miguel
Balboa reached the eastern coast of the Pacific Ocean in 1513. He strode into the water wearing his full armor and claimed the whole sea for Spain. In fact, Portuguese mariners had already sailed into the Pacific Ocean from its western coast in Asia in 1511.

Chucunaque River
Balboa sailed along the coast from Darién and up the Chucunaque River at the start of his journey across the narrowest part of the Isthmus of Panama.

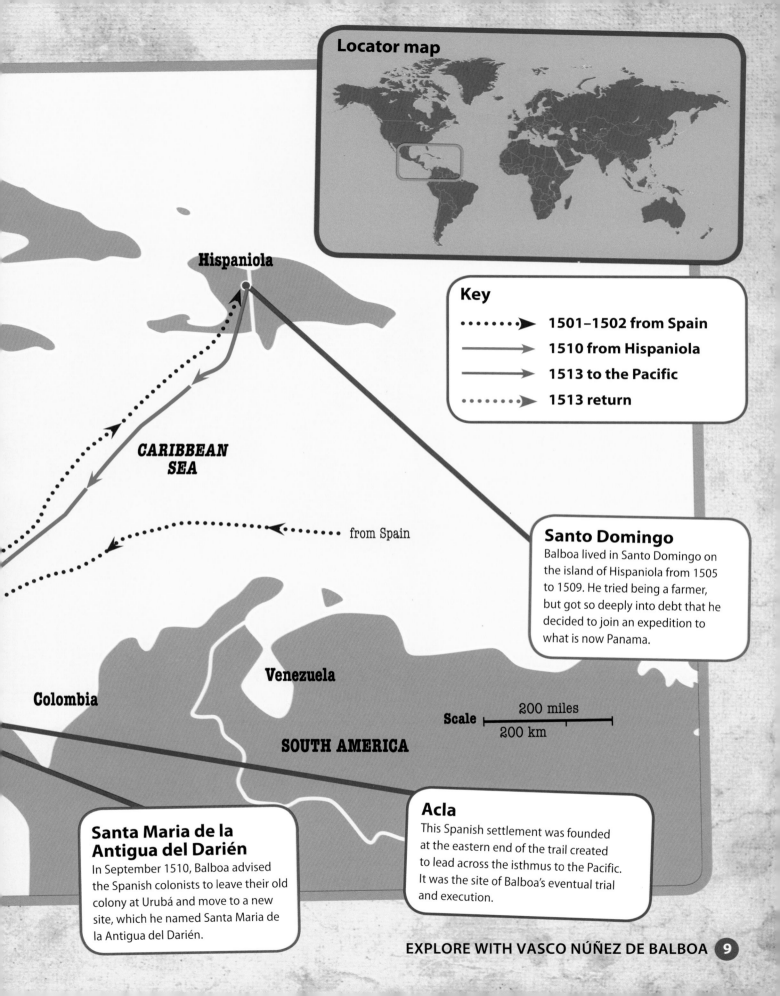

Locator map

Key

· · · · · · · ▶ 1501–1502 from Spain
──────▶ 1510 from Hispaniola
──────▶ 1513 to the Pacific
· · · · · · · ▶ 1513 return

Hispaniola

CARIBBEAN SEA

from Spain

Venezuela

Colombia

Scale ├─ 200 miles ─┤
├─ 200 km ─┤

SOUTH AMERICA

Santo Domingo
Balboa lived in Santo Domingo on the island of Hispaniola from 1505 to 1509. He tried being a farmer, but got so deeply into debt that he decided to join an expedition to what is now Panama.

Santa Maria de la Antigua del Darién
In September 1510, Balboa advised the Spanish colonists to leave their old colony at Urubá and move to a new site, which he named Santa Maria de la Antigua del Darién.

Acla
This Spanish settlement was founded at the eastern end of the trail created to lead across the isthmus to the Pacific. It was the site of Balboa's eventual trial and execution.

Meet the Crew

While there were many people who admired and supported Vasco Núñez de Balboa, there were also some who were jealous of his success.

Leoncico

Balboa was accompanied by his dog, a large bloodhound named Leoncico. He was named for his tawny color, which was like the coat of a lion. In battle, he was trained to attack enemy warriors.

CACICA

+ **Daughter of a chief**

+ **A loyal partner**

Careta was a wealthy Indigenous *cacique*, or chief, who befriended and helped the Spaniards. Balboa eventually married Careta's daughter, Cacica (right). Cacica was initially very loyal to Balboa. She warned him when 5,000 indigenous warriors were plotting to attack him. However, when Balboa tortured her brother to gain more information about the plot, Cacica turned against Balboa.

A GREEDY RULER

★ **King Ferdinand II**

The Spanish king who backed the **conquistadors'** exploration of Central America was crafty and greedy. He hoped his men would find gold and other treasures. He wanted to make the Spanish royal treasury as wealthy as possible, because that would make the country more powerful in Europe.

PEDRO ARIAS DÁVILA

+ Jealous rival

In 1514, King Ferdinand sent Pedro Arias Dávila to replace Balboa as the leader of Darién. The king had not yet received news about Balboa's discovery of the Pacific. Pedrarias, as Arias Dávila was known, was a power-hungry nobleman. He was jealous of Balboa's popularity in Darién. Pedrarias himself was not well liked in the colony and treated Indigenous peoples harshly (below). He feared Balboa would report his failings to the king. To get rid of his rival, Pedrarias eventually had Balboa executed after trying him for treason.

FRANCISCO PIZARRO

☛ **Former friend**

☛ **Famous conquistador**

Francisco Pizarro (above) was in Balboa's expedition that crossed the Isthmus of Panama to reach the Pacific Ocean. He later betrayed Balboa by arresting him in 1519 by order of Pedrarias. Pizarro led his own expedition to Peru in 1532, where he overthrew the Inca Empire and founded a new Spanish capital, Lima.

Check Out the Ride

As much as possible, the Spaniards in Panama traveled by ship or on horseback, but in the thick vegetation of the rain forest, they sometimes simply had to walk.

FAST SHIPS

+ Boats for exploring

+ Also popular with pirates!

The Spaniards used brigantines to explore the coast and rivers of Panama. Brigantines (right) had flat bottoms, which made them suitable for shallow waters. The ships were named for brigands, or pirates. Pirates often used brigantines because they were fast and easy to control.

TRAVEL UPDATE

Get Used to Horses!

★ When traveling in the Spanish Empire in the Americas, horses are useful for their strength and **stamina** (left). Indigenous peoples had never seen horses before the conquistadors brought them to the Americas for the first time. They found the huge animals frightening, which gave the Spaniards an advantage in any fighting.

GOING ON FOOT

- A long walk
- Challenging journey

When Balboa and his troops crossed the Isthmus of Panama, they sailed part way up the Chucunaque River, but they had to make their way through dense jungles by foot (below). The journey took three weeks. The men traveled only 7 to 10 miles (11 to 16 km) each day. Many Spaniards did not survive the trip. They died from sickness or were killed in fighting against Indigenous peoples who tried to stop the Spaniards entering their territory.

My Explorer Journal

★ **Imagine that you are Balboa. Write an advertisement to try to recruit men to make the journey through the rain forest. List the qualities you think they will need.**

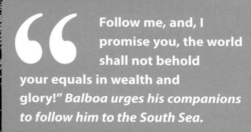

"Follow me, and, I promise you, the world shall not behold your equals in wealth and glory!" *Balboa urges his companions to follow him to the South Sea.*

DUGOUT CANOES

★ **Made from tree trunks**

★ **Used by indigenous people**

The Indigenous peoples in Panama made dugout canoes (left) from the trunks of ceiba trees. They hollowed out the inside of the log and shaped the outside so that they were stable in the water. It could take months to complete a single canoe. The rowers often decorated their oars with pearls.

Solve It With Science

The Spaniards used the latest European technology to their advantage, including wearing armor and using gunpowder weapons to scare their opponents.

Armor

The Spaniards wore metal armor for protection. Most soldiers wore a crested metal helmet and a corselet, which covered the torso. Some men wore full suits of armor, which also included pieces of metal to cover the thighs and the lower legs.

GUNPOWDER WEAPONS

★ **Frightening sounds**

The conquistadors carried gunpowder weapons from Europe. They included cannons and a long gun, called an arquebus (right). The weapons were not very accurate, but they frightened Indigenous people with their noise, flames, and smoke. The guns were so heavy they had to be rested on a pole when they were fired. They took a long time to load, and soldiers always had to carry a lighted **wick** ready to fire them.

FEAT OF ENDURANCE

☛ **Building new brigantines**

☛ **A staggering load**

Wanting to explore the Pacific Ocean, Balboa ordered his soldiers and local people to carry heavy equipment across the Isthmus of Panama. He wanted to build four new brigantines on the Pacific coast. His crew cut down tall trees for wood. They only managed to complete two ships. Pests called sea worms ate through the wood of the other two vessels.

FAMOUS NAVIGATOR

+ Charting a course

+ Putting America on the maps

When Balboa sailed to the Americas with Rodrigo de Bastidas in 1500, the navigator was Juan de la Cosa. De la Cosa had already made the voyage three times, including with Christopher Columbus. He used **dead reckoning** to estimate the distance the ships had sailed, and a **compass** to check the direction in which they were sailing. He also used the position of the stars and planets to navigate. De la Cosa drew the first map to show the American continent (below).

My Explorer Journal

★ **Imagine that you are Juan de la Cosa, and you are mapping a place that has never been mapped before. What sort of features do you think would be most useful to include on your map?**

SHIPBUILDING

★ **Skilled workers**

★ **Build boats**

Balboa was the first Spaniard to build ships in the New World. Near the Pacific coast, his men cut down trees (above) to split into flat planks. **Shipwrights** and carpenters built a timber frame for the hull. They then covered the frame with overlapping planks. Finally, they filled any cracks with plant fibers or tar to make sure no water seeped in.

Did you know ?

One of the most important members of any expedition was the carpenter. He needed to be able to make anything out of wood, from homes and fortifications to bridges or whole ships.

Hanging at Home

Life in the colony at Darién was difficult for the Spaniards, and conditions were not much easier when Balboa and his men went exploring.

Did you know ?

When Balboa was away from Darién, **mutineers** tried to seize the gold in the **treasury**. Other colonists stopped them. The colonists sent a message asking Balboa to return to reclaim control as governor.

LIFE AT DARIÉN

☞ **No great comfort**

☞ **And not much food either!**

Conditions for the Spaniards at Santa Maria de la Antigua del Darién were difficult. The colony was built in a valley, which trapped the heat of the sun. There were few breezes to cool the air. The Spaniards planted vegetable gardens, but there was often not enough food. If the corn harvest failed (above), many colonists went hungry. They begged in the streets for food.

GETTING COMFORTABLE

+ A chance to relax

When Balboa and his men arrived at the village ruled by the cacique Abebeida, they decided to stay for a few days. They anchored their brigantine on the river and spent their time relaxing in **hammocks** in the shade of palm trees. They enjoyed the food and drink they forced the local people to provide. It was such a relaxing time that Balboa's men were unhappy when he decided it was time to continue their expedition.

LIFE IN CAMP

★ Indigenous villages

★ Comfortable places to stay

When they were away from Santa Maria de la Antigua del Darién, Balboa and his men often forced the Indigenous peoples to allow them to stay in their villages. The Spaniards slept in hammocks. They also simply took any food and drink they found. This included meat, wine made from the sap of palm trees (below), and a type of beer made from corn.

POOR RECEPTION

★ Sleeping in a hut

Pedrarias arrived in Darién in 1515 to become the new governor. He was disappointed not to find a city of gold and riches as he had imagined. He and his wife, Doña Isabela, arrived at a colony of thatched huts and dirt roads. Pedrarias was a noble who was used to luxury. He was upset when Balboa greeted him with a vegetarian meal, which was all there was to eat in Darién at the time. He was even more upset to discover that he had to live in a thatched hut, like everyone else.

 Weather Forecast

TERRIBLE CLIMATE!

Balboa and his men struggled with the heat and intense humidity of Panama. In the rainy season, there were also frequent tropical storms. At times on the journey across the isthmus, the rain fell so heavily that the explorers could not see where they were going. Many became exhausted, and their health suffered as a result.

Meeting and Greeting

Balboa tried to maintain friendly relations with Indigenous peoples, but it was not always possible. Some groups were suspicious of the Spaniards and hostile toward them.

THE CARIBS

- Fierce warriors
- Used poisoned arrows

Of all the Indigenous peoples who lived near the colony at Darién, the fiercest were the Caribs. They lived on the eastern shore of the Urabá gulf, where they survived by catching fish from the sea (above). The Carib were known for being fierce warriors, and fought using poisoned arrows. The Spaniards had moved to Darién because of constant Carib attacks on their original colony nearby.

FRIENDLY CACIQUE

- Help along the way
- Sharing food and shelter

Balboa and his men met many Indigenous people. The leaders of these groups were called *caciques*, or chiefs. At a place called Coyba, they met Careta. He treated the Spaniards well, even though they wanted to attack his village in search of gold. Careta and Balboa eventually became friends and helped one another. Balboa married Careta's daughter, Cacica, but later fell out with her.

COMOGRE

+ A powerful leader

+ Useful information

The cacique of the territory next to Careta's was named Comogre. He ruled 10,000 subjects. Comogre's territory included part of the route across the Isthmus of Panama. The Spaniards were amazed by Comogre's home (right). The large house was divided into different sections, including markets and shops, and a place to house the bodies of his dead ancestors. It was Comogre's son who first told Balboa and his men about the Pacific Ocean, which set them on their quest to find it.

Did you know ?

Most conquistadors treated Indigenous peoples harshly. Most Spaniards were only interested in finding treasures. They were from poor families in Spain and were in the Americas to make their fortunes.

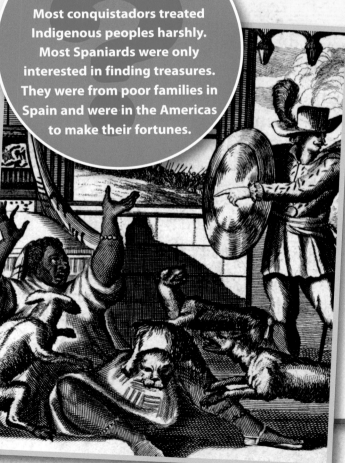

HOSTILE ENCOUNTERS

☛ **Fighting local people**

☛ **Taking treasure**

Balboa was less hostile to Indigenous peoples than some other conquistadors. However, he was still eager to find gold and to claim new territory for Spain. Like other conquistadors, Balboa did not respect the fact that the territory already belonged to the Indigenous people of Panama. When they tried to resist, the Spaniards fought them with guns and swords, and used their dogs to attack individuals (left). The local caciques often had little choice but to help the Spaniards, and to give them any gold, silver, or pearls they owned.

Peoples of Panama

The Indigenous peoples Balboa met had lived on their land for a long time. Their traditions and ways of doing things were different from the way people lived in Spain.

SOCIAL STRUCTURE

+ Born to be leaders

The caciques who led each group of lindigenous people in Panama had great power. They also enjoyed privileges that other members of their groups did not have. They lived in larger houses, for example. They were allowed to have more than one wife, while other men could only have one. Balboa tried to establish good relationships with many caciques to help make his explorations easier.

TWO STYLES OF HOME

☛ **Living in groups**

☛ **Homes in the trees**

The Indigenous people Balboa and his men met lived in two main types of houses. The *bohio* (right) was built on a frame made of cane, with a steep thatched roof made of grass, palm leaves, or other materials. It was common for several families to share one house. Other people lived in houses built in the trees or on cane stilts. These homes, called *barbacoas*, were entered using tall ladders. Being high up protected people from flooding and wild animals.

TRAVEL UPDATE

Hire a Guide!

★ One of the best ways to explore new land is with a knowledgeable guide. Balboa and his men often depended on Indigenous guides. The cacique Poncha, for example, provided the guides for the difficult journey across the Isthmus of Panama. Without them, there is no guarantee Balboa would have been successful.

My Explorer Journal

★ Imagine that you are a Idigenous cacique in Panama. Do you think you would welcome Balboa and his men or be suspicious of them? Give your reasons.

AREITO

☞ A show of hospitality

☞ Making music

Some Indigenous peoples welcomed the Spaniards with ceremonies and a type of dance called the *areito*. People sang while musicians played drums made from hollow logs and rattles made from **gourds**. The ceremonies and music may have also been a way for people to worship their ancestors.

DECORATED PEOPLE

★ Too hot for clothes

Because of the hot and humid weather, many Indigenous men and boys went naked or wore short **loincloths**, while the women wore cotton skirts. Men painted their skin with a red-orange dye made from the seeds of the achiote tree, or decorated themselves with tattoos. Traditional peoples in the region still use body paint (right). Men and women also wore feather headdresses and gold jewelry, and used decorations made from seashells in their noses and ears.

I Love Nature

The climate and landscape the Spaniards found in Panama were very different from what they were used to. There were many new plants and animals.

EDIBLE ROOT

☛ **Important food source**

☛ **Used to make flatbread**

Cassava roots provided Indigenous peoples with an important source of **carbohydrates**. People dug up the woody roots and ground them into flour that they used to make flatbread. If not prepared properly, cassava can be poisonous. The root must be washed well before it can be eaten. Indigenous peoples showed the Spaniards how to find and prepare cassava, which became an important food in

 Weather Forecast

RAIN AND MORE RAIN!

Rain forests get their name from the heavy rainfall that keeps them hot and humid. The moisture supports many species of plants, such as mosses and ferns at ground level, shrubs and vines in the understory, and tall trees that form the forest canopy. The forests are also home to many animals, including monkeys, anteaters, a giant rodent called the capybara (right), plus jaguars and pumas.

A GIANT TREE

+ Tallest in the rain forest

+ Used to make canoes

Ceiba trees are some of the tallest in the tropical rain forest. They can grow up to 200 feet (60 meters) tall. Their upper branches curve down in an umbrella-like canopy, and they provide homes to many animals and birds. Indigenous people used their thick trunks to make dug-out canoes. The ancient Mayan people of Mexico and Guatemala believed that ceiba trees connected heaven and earth, because they were so tall.

> They are the most perfect and beautiful pearls in all the world! None like these have I seen, even at the court of my queen." *Doña Isabela describes the pearls Balboa found.*

LIVING OFF THE LAND

★ **Keeping gardens**

While Balboa's colony in Darién faced many problems, it did have rich soil that made it ideal for gardening. The Spaniards soon learned to grow their own food, including potatoes and corn, although the crops often failed in the heat. Their most prized fruit was the pineapple. The fruit was not available in Spain at the time.

Fortune Hunting

Like many Spaniards who headed to the New World, Balboa dreamed of becoming wealthy. He found more treasures than many other conquistadors.

GOLDEN CASTILE

+ Rivers of gold

Balboa found gold easily in Panama. In 1513, he wrote a letter to the king of Spain describing how gold flowed in the rivers. Even though Balboa's account was an exaggeration, it caused the king to give the colony of Darién a new name: Castile the Golden. This reputation caused many more Spaniards to travel to Panama. The Spanish often took gold from the Indigenous people, sometimes by befriending them but also by force. Gold was sent back to Spain, where it was put in the royal treasury (above).

A GOLDEN TEMPLE

★ **A place of worship**

★ **But does it even exist?**

One of the stories Balboa heard in Panama was that Indigenous peoples had built a golden temple to worship a goddess who protected them. The temple was said to be in a region called Dobaybe. According to the stories, the temple contained a golden idol and was full of gold left there by worshipers. Although Balboa searched for the temple, he never managed to find it.

ROUTE TO THE EAST

- Priceless antiquities
- Revealing the past

Balboa hoped to find a westward route to Asia, to countries like India, Indonesia, and China. Muslim traders controlled the trade routes between Europe and Asia, and the Spanish wanted access to silks, spices (right), and other goods from Asia. When Balboa reached the Pacific Ocean in 1513, he believed he may have found a sea route to Asia.

STORIES OF GOLD

+ Motivated to find gold

Like the other conquistadors, Balboa was driven to explore by the desire for gold. He dreamed of becoming very rich. The son of the cacique Comogre told Balboa about people on the coast of the Pacific Ocean who had so much gold they used it for jewelry and statues (left), ate off golden plates, and drank from golden cups. It was the promise of gold that convinced Balboa to lead the difficult expedition across the Isthmus of Panama.

TRAVEL UPDATE

The King's Fifth

★ Spaniards visting the New World should remember King Ferdinand's huge greed for gold. If any Spanish explorers found gold, they had to send one-fifth of it back to Spain to the king. Balboa always kept the king's fifth set aside, and now and then put it on a boat sailing for Spain.

This Isn't What It Said in the Brochure!

Balboa faced many challenges, such as bad weather and dangerous enemies. However, the biggest danger came from his fellow Spaniards, who plotted against him.

Pride

Balboa's trip to the Pearl Islands was an example of how the Spaniards sometimes suffered from their pride. They paid the price of thinking they knew better than locals, who warned them not to sail.

STORM AHEAD

+ Spaniards nearly drown

Balboa demanded canoes from local people on the Pacific coast in order to sail to the Pearl Islands (right). Ignoring advice, he set to sea and was caught in a huge storm that threatened to sink the canoes. The crew landed on a small island, but during the night the rising tide threatened to drown them. They repaired the canoes the next day but had lost all their provisions. They had to make a difficult journey back to the shore.

TOUGH ENVIRONMENT

- Hunger and sickness
- Losing men in battle

Balboa and his men struggled with heat, hunger, and illness in Panama. Their heavy armor made tasks such as raising a cross to mark the sighting of the Pacific (left) exhausting. While the Spanish killed many Indigenous peoples in battles, they also lost many of their own men. The Spaniards died of sickness or were killed by poison-tipped arrows or spears in bitter fighting.

BAD TIDINGS

- An enemy tells lies
- A possible trial

Balboa was a strong leader, so he was happy to receive orders making him the temporary governor of Darién. At the same time, however, he received a letter from Spain. Balboa's enemy, Martin Fernandez de Encisco, had told the king that Balboa had rejected royal authority. The story was not true, but Balboa was upset to learn that he could be put on trial for **treason**.

GOING HUNGRY

+ Rotten food

In 1514, Pedrarias (below) arrived in Darién to become its new leader. He arrived with 22 ships and 1,500 settlers. He and his crew soon found that the bacon, biscuits, and other food they had taken with them had rotted on the journey. Not long after that, a building that stored food in the colony burned down. In the end, more than 700 Spaniards died from starvation and sickness in Darién in just one month.

TRAVEL UPDATE

Difficult Journey

★ One key lesson for explorers is to get your priorities right when packing. After Balboa and his men visited the Pacific Ocean, they carried back so many pearls, gold, and other treasures that they could not carry enough food. For some men, such financial greed was fatal. They died of starvation on the trip back through the rain forest to Darién.

End of the Road

Balboa had many successes during this life as an explorer. However, his achievements made other people jealous—and cost Balboa his life.

A GOLDEN EMPIRE

- ☞ Hearing about the Inca people
- ☞ A wealthy civilization

A cacique named Tumaco told the Spaniards about a land to the south where people had lots of gold. Among the Spaniards who heard the story was Francisco Pizarro. He was inspired to go to find this land, which turned out to be the Inca **Empire** of Peru. Pizarro finally traveled to Peru in 1532. He met the ruler, Atahualpa (right), and took him captive. The Spaniards overthrew the Inca Empire the following year.

THE NEW GOVERNOR

- ☞ A cruel leader
- ☞ Difficult relationships

When Pedrarias arrived in Darién in 1514, he and Balboa tried to get along. However, it was a difficult relationship because Pedrarias was jealous of Balboa. Balboa had a reputation as a fair governor and was famous as the man who had discovered the South Sea (right). Pedrarias was determined to destroy Balboa's reputation. He also treated the Indigenous people harshly, which strained relations in the region.

TREACHERY

★ A terrible lie

★ Trouble begins

As part of his efforts to get along with Pedrarias, Balboa agreed to marry Maria, Pedrarias's daughter. Although Balboa never met Maria, who was back in Europe, he had to end his relationship with his wife, Cacica. Cacica complained to a Spanish admirer, Andrés Garabito. To get back at Balboa, Garabito lied to Pedrarias that Balboa was planning a secret voyage to Peru to claim the Inca Empire for himself. An angry Pedrarias decided to take revenge.

ARREST AND TRIAL

★ Pedrarias gets revenge

Pedrarias wrote Balboa, inviting him to a meeting. However, when Balboa arrived, he was arrested by Francisco Pizarro on the orders of Pedrarias. Balboa was put on trial for rebelling against the Spanish government. Witnesses lied about his plot to travel to Peru. Balboa was found guilty and sentenced to death.

EXECUTION

+ Balboa is beheaded

+ Dead at age 43

On January 12, 1519, Balboa and four of his friends were led into the main square of a settlement named Acla. Pedrarias was watching from the crowd. Each man was beheaded (below). Balboa's head was displayed in the square for several days.

Did you know ?

Pedrarias abandoned the colony at Darién in 1519 and founded a new capital at what is now Panama City. He remained governor until 1527, when he became governor of Nicaragua.

GLOSSARY

bribe To dishonestly persuade someone to do something, usually by paying them

carbohydrates Substances contained in food that are broken down by the body to provide energy

colony An overseas settlement or area ruled by another country

compass A device with a magnetized needle that points north, used for navigation

conquistadors Spanish adventurers who conquered South America and Mexico

dead reckoning A method of navigation based on figuring out how far a ship has sailed in a certain direction

empire A large area ruled by the same ruler

fatigue A feeling of extreme tiredness

gourds Large, fleshy fruits with hard shells that are used to hold liquids or as musical instruments

hammock A bed that hangs from hooks at either end

humid A climate that is warm and damp

indigenous Native to a particular place

isthmus A narrow strip of land with sea on either side, forming a link between two larger areas of land

loincloth A garment for men formed by a long piece of cloth wrapped around the hips

mutineers Military personnel who rebel against their senior officers

nobility The traditional aristocracy or social elite of a country

notary A legal official who is authorized to draw up contracts

prospects Chances for success in the future

shipwrights Craftspeople who are skilled at making ships and boats

stamina The ability to make a continuous physical effort

thatched Having a roof of straw, grass, or leaves

treason The crime of betraying your own country

treasury A place where a ruler or government stores its valuable treasure

understory A layer of trees and shrubs that grows beneath the tallest plants of the rain forest

wick A small strip of slow-burning material used to set fire to things

---

Vasco Núñez de Balboa is born to a poor but noble family in Spain.

Balboa settles as a farmer in Santo Domingo, a Spanish colony in Hispaniola, where he soon gets into debt.

September: Balboa recommends moving the Spanish colony from Urubá to Santa Maria de la Antigua del Darién.

September: King Ferdinand II of Spain makes Balboa temporary governor of Darién. Balboa begins a campaign to force local peoples to hand over gold and other treasures.

c. 1475   1500   1505   1509   1510   1511

With few prospects in Spain, Balboa joins an expedition to Colombia led by Rodrigo de Bastidas.

To escape his debts, Balboa stows away on a voyage to Colombia led by Martín Fernández de Enciso.

March: When the colonists despose Enciso as leader of Darién, Balboa takes his place.

ON THE WEB

https://allaboutexplorers.com/explorers/balboa/
A page about Balboa and his journey to the Pacific Ocean.

exploration.marinersmuseum.org/subject/vasco-de-balboa/
An account of the expedition from the Mariners' Museum.

www.timetoast.com/timelines/86085
A timeline of Balboa's life and career as an explorer.

explorers.mrdonn.org/balboa.html
The Mr. Donn pages have a biography of Balboa for young readers.

kids.nationalgeographic.com/explore/countries/panama/
A National Geographic site about Panama, the country that Balboa helped to develop.

BOOKS

Gunderson, Jessica. *Conquistadors* (Fearsome Fighters). Creative Education, 2012.

Nagelhout, Ryan. *Vasco Núñez de Balboa: First European to Reach the Pacific Ocean from the New World* (Spotlight on Explorers and Colonization). Rosen Young Adult, 2016.

Petrie, Kristin. *Vasco Núñez de Balboa* (Explorers). Checkerboard Books, 2007.

Vail, Martha. *Exploring the Pacific* (Discovery and Exploration). Chelsea House Publications, 2009.

September 1: Having heard tales of a great ocean to the south, Balboa sets out to sail along the coast to the narrowest part of the Isthmus of Panama.

January 14: Balboa returns to Darién and announces his discovery.

Balboa carries equipment across Panama to build ships in order to explore the Pacific coast.

January 12: After a court finds Balboa guilty, he is beheaded in Acla.

1513   **1514**   **1517**   **1518**   **1517**

September 25: Balboa climbs a mountain in Darién and sees the Pacific Ocean. A few days later he reaches the coast.

June: Pedro Arias Dávila arrives in Dairén with 2,000 colonists and takes control of the colony.

Worried that Balboa will turn the king against him, Pedrarias invites him to a meeting, where Balboa is arrested.

INDEX